THE MOON FILES

MINING
THE MOON

Diane Lindsey Reeves

Lerner Publications ◆ Minneapolis

A big thank you to Evan Clasen for his encouragement and interest in this project.

Lerner Publications Company
An imprint of Lerner Publishing Group, Inc.
241 First Avenue North
Minneapolis, MN 55401 USA

For reading levels and more information, look up this title at www.lernerbooks.com.

Main body text set in Aptifer Sans LT Pro.
Typeface provided by Linotype.

Library of Congress Cataloging-in-Publication Data

Names: Reeves, Diane Lindsey, 1959–author.
Title: Mining the moon / Diane Lindsey Reeves.
Description: Minneapolis, MN : Lerner Publications, [2024] | Series: Alternator books. The moon files | Includes bibliographical references and index. | Audience: Ages 8–12 | Audience: Grades 4–6 | Summary: "The moon is home to a treasure trove of metals, minerals, and other natural resources. Explore how space agencies are looking to safely and ethically mine the moon and what this means for the future"—Provided by publisher.
Identifiers: LCCN 2023049549 (print) | LCCN 2023049550 (ebook) | ISBN 9798765625613 (library binding) | ISBN 9798765629826 (paperback) | ISBN 9798765637920 (epub)
Subjects: LCSH: Lunar mining—Juvenile literature. | Moon—Juvenile literature.
Classification: LCC TN291.35 .R44 2024 (print) | LCC TN291.35 (ebook) | DDC 622.0999/1—dc23/eng/20231107

LC record available at https://lccn.loc.gov/2023049549
LC ebook record available at https://lccn.loc.gov/2023049550

Manufactured in the United States of America
1 – CG – 7/15/24

Note to Readers: Images showing people living on the moon come from the imaginations of artists. They reflect ideas about how things might someday be.

TABLE OF CONTENTS

The moon is rich with important minerals and metals.

INTRODUCTION

LUNAR MINERALS

When astronauts have visited the moon, they have brought back rocks for scientists to study. Scientists were surprised to discover that moon rocks are very much like Earth rocks. They have many of the same important minerals.

Scientists think the moon is full of resources that are in short supply on Earth. They believe these resources could make life better on Earth for centuries to come.

There are still more questions than answers about how to mine the moon. There are important questions about whether or not humans should even try. But it is exciting to imagine how it could happen!

Astronauts from Apollo 11 gather moon rocks.

CHAPTER 1

MOON TREASURE HUNT

Research has shown that the moon is rich in important resources. The National Aeronautics and Space Administration (NASA) estimates that the moon has natural resources that

NASA's Moon Mineralogy Mapper shows a moon rich in mineral deposits.

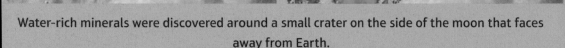

Water-rich minerals were discovered around a small crater on the side of the moon that faces away from Earth.

are worth hundreds of billions of dollars. This includes metals, minerals, and elements. These resources are also found on Earth. But some are very rare and hard to find on our planet.

The first clues about these resources were found in moon rocks. Astronauts from Apollo missions brought them back from the moon from 1969 to 1972. The rocks were collected during spacewalks by the first astronauts to visit the moon.

When studying these rocks, scientists found evidence of common minerals such as basalt, iron, quartz, and silicon on the moon. These types of minerals are used to make things such as buildings, windows, and solar panels.

In 2020, NASA confirmed that there is water on the moon. This means the moon could supply water used for drinking and oxygen. It could even be used for rocket fuel. This discovery might make it possible for humans to spend more time on the moon. It could also provide a way to fuel long missions to Mars.

Mountain Pass, California, is where the largest rare-earth element mine in the US is located.

Titanium is used to make useful products such as golf clubs.

Rare Earth Metals

The moon is home to some very rare resources. They are called rare earth metals. Some metals such as neodymium and lanthanum are hard to find on Earth. But there are lots of those metals on the moon. These rare metals are used in technologies like speakers, smartphones, batteries, and camera lenses. Other useful metals found on the moon include aluminum and titanium.

Scientists are looking at the possibility of mining helium-3 on the moon. Helium-3 is a gas made by the solar winds of the sun. Earth's magnetic field blocks it from getting here. This magnetic field is created by the motion of red-hot iron in Earth's core. It protects the planet from the sun's radiation. The moon has no magnetic field, which means there is lots of helium-3.

LIQUEFIED HYDROGEN
FLAMMABLE GAS

NASA uses hydrogen as fuel for space vehicles.

HYDROGEN

The fossil fuels the world depends on now won't last forever. Helium-3 could replace fossil fuels as a clean and powerful fuel source. Scientists are working out how to get this gas from the moon to Earth.

H₂O BLAST OFF!

Water, or H_2O, is a mix of hydrogen and oxygen. Using a special process, it is possible to split water molecules into oxygen gas and hydrogen gas. Hydrogen is used as light and rocket fuel. Space agencies are trying to figure out how astronauts could convert water into hydrogen fuel on the moon. This could be used to refuel rockets for deep space exploration.

Coal is a fossil fuel used to generate electrical power.

Miners must dig deep to find the minerals they are looking for.

CHAPTER 2

FROM MOON TO EARTH

There are a lot of steps to mining. First, you have to find areas of rocks that are full of minerals. Then, you have to figure out a safe way to remove it from the rocks around it. This often involves lots of expensive equipment and large vehicles.

People must be hired and trained to do the work. They must follow many rules and processes. All this happens when mining resources on Earth.

Moon mining has even more steps. There are 238,855 miles (384,400 km) between the moon and Earth. How can you move large amounts of minerals and metals from there to here? It is a huge challenge. But it's one that scientists are busy trying to figure out.

It is a long way from the moon to Earth.

What if a moon base looked something like this?

"What If" Questions

Right now, many ideas are still in the "what if" phase. For example, what if we could build a moon base camp where humans could live and work for long periods of time? This would be a big step toward getting ready to mine the moon.

What if we could use reusable rockets to transport people and materials from the moon to Earth? NASA's Space Shuttle was history's first reusable spacecraft. Now private companies such as SpaceX are making rockets that are less costly. These rockets can be used multiple times to move people and equipment. Reusable rockets use less fuel. That makes them better for the environment.

What if we could use 3-D printers to make products on the moon? This would end the need to move huge amounts of raw materials back to Earth. Instead, the actual products would be made on the moon and shipped back to Earth.

A reusable human lander called Starship is being built by SpaceX.

University students compete to create lunar robots for NASA.

Robots on the Moon

What if we could use robots to mine materials? Using artificial intelligence, robots can be made to do almost anything. Robots could handle the routine, physical tasks of mining. Fewer humans would be needed to work in dangerous situations.

Scientists all over the world are working to overcome challenges like these. There are no easy answers. But landing humans on the moon wasn't easy either. Scientists made it happen through creative problem-solving and teamwork.

Successfully sending the first humans to the moon inspires scientists to solve new challenges.

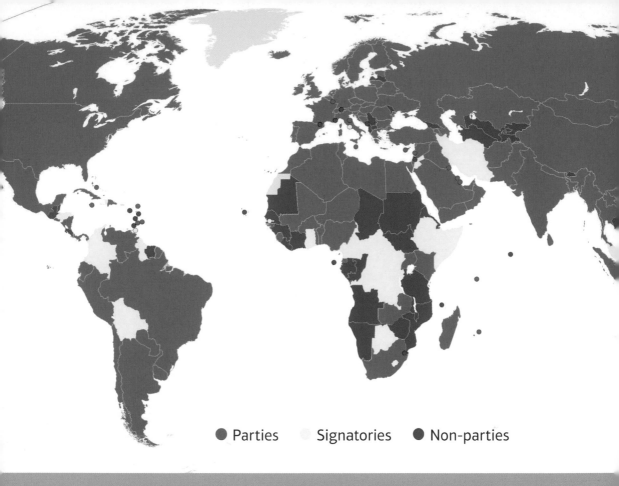

● Parties   ● Signatories   ● Non-parties

Countries all over the world agreed to the Outer Space Treaty.

CHAPTER 3

RESPONSIBLE MINING

Space experts are figuring out how to mine the moon. Others wonder if we should even try. After all, who owns the moon's resources?

According to the Outer Space Treaty, no country or individual is allowed to own the moon. This important international agreement was made in 1967. This was two years before the United States landed the first humans on the moon. The treaty was signed by more than 100 nations, including the US. They agreed that all countries are free to explore space. They also agreed to avoid causing damage in space.

The International Space Station has proven that astronauts from different countries can work together in space.

Sharing the Moon

The Outer Space Treaty was signed long before anyone realized the moon is so rich in resources. It was before Earth's fossil fuels were nearly used up. The US, Japan, India, China, the United Arab Emirates, the European Union, and others are interested in using those resources. So are many private companies. But everyone has to decide how to mine those resources fairly.

Countries who sign the Artemis Accords agree to peaceful space exploration.

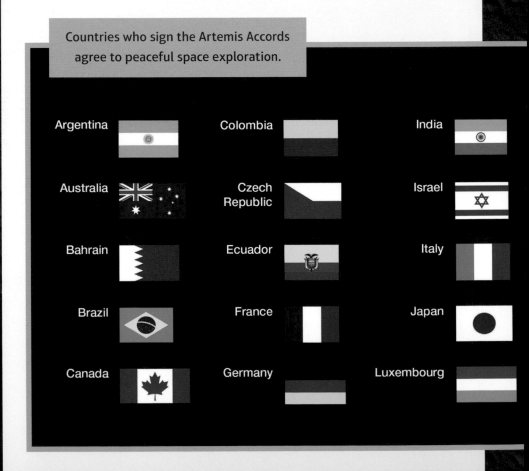

Argentina		Colombia		India	
Australia		Czech Republic		Israel	
Bahrain		Ecuador		Italy	
Brazil		France		Japan	
Canada		Germany		Luxembourg	

The Artemis Accords is a first step in that direction. It is an agreement drafted by the US in 2020. So far, many countries have agreed to follow it. This includes Australia, Canada, Italy, Japan, Luxembourg, the United Arab Emirates, and the United Kingdom. The agreement updates some space rules. It also states that everyone must come in peace and shares guidelines for how to work together. Space exploration must be open for all who wish to participate.

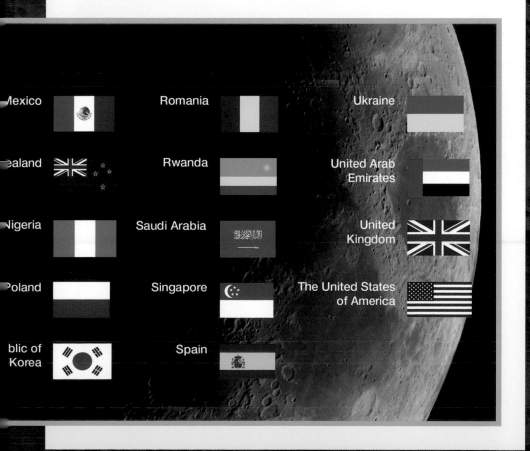

Mexico

Romania

Ukraine

ealand

Rwanda

United Arab
Emirates

Nigeria

Saudi Arabia

United
Kingdom

Poland

Singapore

The United States
of America

blic of
Korea

Spain

Safety First

Keeping humans safe is another big ethical concern. Traveling to the moon has many risks. The longest crewed mission to the moon lasted twelve days. To start mining, people would need to stay much longer than that. There is research to be done and mining operations to set up.

Many other functions also require human effort on the moon for long periods of time. Where would humans live? What would they eat and drink? How could they manage being away from Earth for so long? These questions must be answered before mining can begin.

Safety doesn't stop with people. Mining must be done in a way that doesn't damage the moon. The moon's gravity helps hold Earth steady. That way it doesn't wobble on its axis too much. This is just one of the ways the moon helps us survive on Earth.

Scientists do not want to destroy the moon by mining too much.

Lunar resources could help solve big problems on Earth.

Fossil Fuel Process

Time and nature convert fossils into fuels the world uses for energy.

Is mining the moon worth it? Some say, yes, it is. The moon is full of resources that could be used to help humans survive and thrive on Earth. It is up to us to safeguard those riches for many generations to come.

MOON RICHES

NASA experts estimate that the moon's resources are large in number. Even if a metric ton was removed from the moon every day, it would take 220 million years to use just 1 percent of the moon's mass. Experts say that mining would not change the moon's orbit or change the way that gravity causes high and low tides on Earth's oceans.

The Artemis 1 flight test launched aboard the Orion spacecraft with three non-human passengers aboard.

CHAPTER 4

SEARCHING FOR ANSWERS

NASA is not alone in its plans to explore and mine the moon. It is leading a program called Artemis. NASA is working closely with the European Space Agency. Space agencies in Japan, Canada, Israel, Australia, and India are also part of Artemis.

Artemis is an effort to once again land humans on the moon. Multiple missions are planned. Artemis 1 started by sending three manikins into space aboard the Orion spacecraft. These nonhuman passengers were used to test safety features. The mission is helping experts better prepare to keep humans safe.

After a successful 25.5 day mission into deep space, the Orion splashed down in the Pacific Ocean.

The Artemis 2 crew includes the first woman and the first person of color to fly around the moon.

A Mission of Firsts

The Artemis 2 mission will send a human crew farther into space than ever before. The mission is expected to last ten days. Its crew will include the first woman and the first person of color to circle the moon. This mission is meant to pave the way for future moon landings. The astronauts will test new technologies and safety features.

Artemis 3 will take space exploration even further. The plan is to land a crew at the moon's south polar region. During their time on the moon, the crew will do many scientific experiments and take moonwalks to gather samples.

There are plans for Artemis 4 to dock with the Lunar Gateway in 2028. The Gateway will be a space station that orbits the moon.

One step at a time, the overall goal is to make a long-term presence on the moon. This will allow international partners to explore mining the moon. It will also take space exploration one step closer to another huge goal: sending astronauts to Mars.

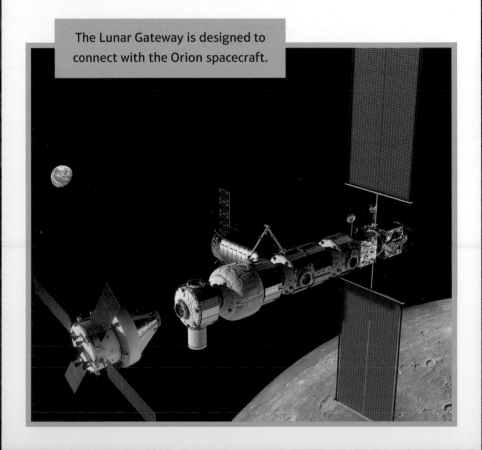

The Lunar Gateway is designed to connect with the Orion spacecraft.

GLOSSARY

3-D printer: a machine used to produce a three-dimensional object layer-by-layer using a computer created design

artificial intelligence: complex computer systems that are programmed to perform tasks that normally require human intelligence

axis: an imaginary line around which an object rotates; the two ends of the Earth's axis are its north and south

ecosystem: made up of living things (like animals and plants) and nonliving things (like rocks and dirt) in an area

ethical: decisions based on what is morally right and honest

fossil fuel: a fuel, such as oil, gas, and coal, made from natural things that were alive in the distant past

helium-3: a light, stable isotope of helium with two protons and one neutron; a trace element found in solar wind

lanthanum: a soft, white rare earth metal found in televisions, energy-saving lamps, and other technologies

neodymium: a silvery-white rare earth metal that is used for coloring glass and ceramics

treaty: a formal written agreement between two or more nations

LEARN MORE

Adelman, Beth. *The Moon's Impact on Our Earth*. Minneapolis: Lerner Publications, 2025.

Britannica Kids: Moon
https://kids.britannica.com/kids/article/Moon/353489

Buxner, Sanlyn Dr., Dr. Pamela Gay, and Dr. Georgiana Kramer. *The Moon*. New York: DK, 2022.

NASA Space Place: Moon
https://spaceplace.nasa.gov/search/moon

National Geographic: Mining
https://education.nationalgeographic.org/resource/mining/

Page, Nathan. *Who Was the First Man on the Moon?: Neil Armstrong*. New York: Penguin Workshop, 2021.

Rajczak, Michael. *Reaching the Moon*. New York: Gareth Stevens, 2021.

Study.com: What Is the Moon Made Of?
https://study.com/academy/lesson/what-is-the-moon-made-of-lesson-for-kids.html

INDEX

PHOTO ACKNOWLEDGMENTS

Image Credits: Interior; Helen Field/Shutterstock, Interior; TB3XNW/Alamy; Interior; titoOnz/Alamy, p. 4; posteriori/iStockphoto, p. 5; NASA Johnson, p. 6; ISRO/NASA/JPL-Caltech/Brown Univ./USGS, p. 7; ISRO/NASA/JPL-Caltech/USGS/Brown Univ, p. 8; NASA Earth Observatory/Allison Nussbaum, p. 9; Billion Photos/Shutterstock, p. 10; NASA/Kim Shiflett, p. 11; Maksim Safaniuk/Shutterstock, p. 12; Lucian Coman/Shutterstock, p. 13; Dima Zel, p. 14; NASA, p. 15; NASA/SpaceX, p. 16; NASA, p. 17; NASA, p. 18; OuterSpace Treaty/Creative Commons, p. 19; Marc Ward/Shutterstock, p. 20-21; NASA, p. 22; NASA; p. 23; Artsiom P/Shutterstock, p. 24; estherpoon, p. 25; angkrit/Shutterstock; p. 26; NASA/Bill Ingalls, p. 27; NASA, p. 28; NASA/Frank Michaux, p. 29; NASA.

Cover: Alan Luk/Adobe.